Bendemolena

A play based on an American folktale
by Edel Wignell   Illustrated by Mini Goss

Series editor: Mark Carthew

ETA Cuisenaire

Characters

Narrator
(Storyteller)

Bendemolena

Mother Cat

Kitten 1

Kitten 2

Kitten 3

Kitten 4

Mr. Horse

Turn to page **21** for Sound and Stage Tips

Bendemolena

Scene 1   What a Noisy House!

Narrator: Once there was a kitten named Bendemolena. Her brothers, sisters, and neighbors ran in and out of the house all day.

Kitten Chorus: In and out, in and out,
Ha, ha, ha!
Follow me, follow me,
Tra, la, la!

Narrator: What a noisy house it was! Bendemolena hated the shouting and the racket. What could she do?

Bendemolena: Here's a shiny pot! I'll put it on my head. (*Pause as she puts the pot on her head.*) Hooray! The noise has gone away! The house is quiet! I'll wear this pot all the time.

Narrator: Soon Mother Cat gathered all her kittens together to tell them about her plan for the day.

Mother Cat: Listen, kittens! I am going to look after my friend Mrs. Tabby, who is sick.

Kitten Chorus: Yes, Mother.

Mother Cat: I'll be away all day, so I won't be able to clean the house and cook your supper.

Kitten 1: Don't worry, Mother. We'll do it.

Kitten 2: When you come home, you'll find a clean house.

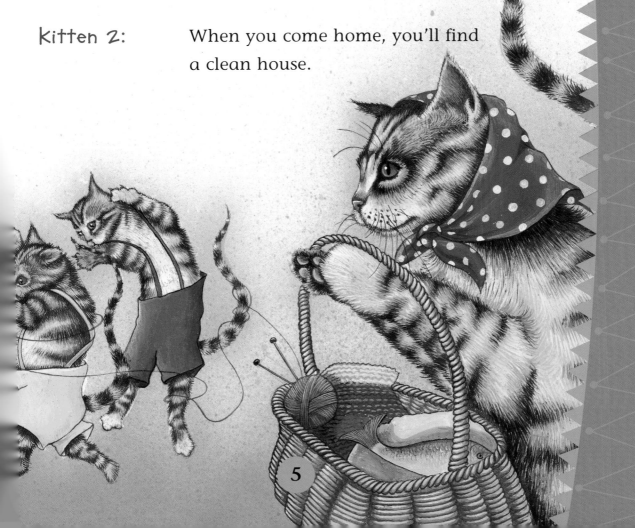

Kitten 3: Supper will be ready.

Kitten 4: We'll look after everything.

Mother Cat: Thank you, my good, helpful kittens! Now, come with me, Bendemolena. You can run messages from Mrs. Tabby's place to your brothers and sisters.

Kitten Chorus: Good-bye, Mother! Good-bye, Bendemolena!

Mother Cat: Good-bye, kittens. Off we go!

6

Scene 2   Fish!

Narrator: Mother Cat and Bendemolena went to Mrs. Tabby's house. Soon it was time for Mother Cat to send a message to the kittens.

Mother Cat: Bendemolena, run home and tell your brothers and sisters it's time to put the fish on to bake.

Bendemolena: Yes, Mother.

Narrator: Bendemolena's ears were under the pot, so she didn't hear her right. The message was mixed up. As she ran, she wondered.

Bendemolena: Did Mother say to soak a dish in the lake, or put a cape on the snake? No, I'm sure she said, "Put soap in the cake."

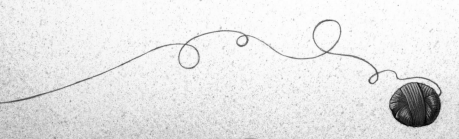

| Narrator: | Arriving home, she gave the message to the kittens. |

| Bendemolena: | Mother wants you to put soap in the cake. |

| Narrator: | The kittens were surprised, but they sang as they grated soap into the cake mix. |

| Kitten Chorus: | Soap in the cake, Soap in the cake! Yes, Mother! Soap in the cake! |

| Narrator: | Meanwhile, Bendemolena hurried back to her mother, who was busy looking after Mrs. Tabby. |

8

Scene 3   Soup!

Narrator: Soon Mother Cat had another message for the kittens.

Mother Cat: Bendemolena, run home and tell your brothers and sisters it's time to put the soup on to heat.

Bendemolena: Yes, Mother.

Narrator: Again, Bendemolena didn't hear her right, so the message was mixed up. As she ran, she wondered.

Bendemolena: Did Mother say to put a boot on the sheets, or try the shoes on your feet? No, I'm sure she said, "Iron the meat."

Narrator: Arriving home, she gave the message to the kittens.

Bendemolena: Mother wants you to iron the meat.

Narrator: The kittens were surprised, but they sang as they took out the iron and the ironing board and ironed the meat.

Kitten Chorus: Iron the meat,
Iron the meat!
Yes, Mother!
Iron the meat!

Narrator: Meanwhile, Bendemolena hurried back to her mother, who was busy looking after Mrs. Tabby.

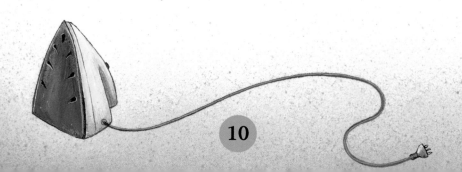

Scene 4   Key!

Narrator: Soon Mother Cat had another message for the kittens.

Mother Cat: Bendemolena, tell your brothers and sisters to be sure to leave the key in the lock.

Bendemolena: Yes, Mother.

Narrator: Once more, Bendemolena didn't hear her right, so the message was mixed up. As she ran, she wondered.

Bendemolena: Did Mother say to put the leaves in the sock, or close the crock if it snows? No, I'm sure she said, "Sew clothes on the clock."

Narrator: Arriving home, she gave the message to the kittens.

Bendemolena: Mother wants you to sew clothes on the clock.

Narrator: The kittens were surprised, but they sang as they found the scissors, needles, and thread and sewed clothes on the clock.

Kitten Chorus: Clothes on the clock,
Clothes on the clock!
Yes, Mother!
Clothes on the clock!

Narrator: Meanwhile, Bendemolena hurried back to her mother, who was busy looking after Mrs. Tabby.

Scene 5   Drink!

Narrator: Soon Mother Cat had another message for the kittens.

Mother Cat: Bendemolena, supper must be nearly ready now. Go and tell your brothers and sisters to make something to drink.

Narrator: For the fourth time, Bendemolena didn't hear her right, so the message was mixed up. As she ran, she wondered.

Bendemolena: Did Mother say to take some ink to the store, or toot the horns while you wink? No, I'm sure she said, "Put a horse in the sink."

Narrator: Arriving home, she gave the message to the kittens.

Bendemolena: Mother wants you to put a horse in the sink.

Narrator: The kittens were surprised, but they sang as they set off up the street.

Kitten Chorus: Horse in the sink,
Horse in the sink!
Yes, Mother!
Horse in the sink!

Narrator: The kittens ran to Mr. Horse, who lived nearby.

Kittens 1 and 2: Mr. Horse, please come to our house.

Kittens 3 and 4: Mother has sent a message. She wants you to stand in the sink.

Mr. Horse: Stand in the sink? Certainly!

Narrator: Everyone hurried back to Bendemolena's house.

Kitten Chorus: Go and come,
Come and go.
What is happening?
Let us know!

Scene 6   How Did This Happen?

Narrator: Just then, Mother Cat and Bendemolena
                 arrived home. Mother Cat looked
                 around, surprised.

Mother Cat: What's happening, kittens? I see:
                 Soap bubbles rising from the cake,
                 Meat on the ironing board
                 that's ready to bake,
                 The clock dressed in pink,
                 And a horse in the sink.
                 How did this happen?

Kitten Chorus: Surprise, surprise!
                 We didn't rest.
                 We got your messages
                 And did our best!

Narrator: Bendemolena was still mixed up.

Narrator: Mother Cat looked at Mr. Horse and the smiling kittens. Then she looked at Bendemolena's head, and she couldn't stay angry.

Mother Cat: The pot! The pot caused the mix-ups. Bendemolena couldn't hear me right. Let's have supper, everyone!

18

Narrator: Mother Cat took the pot off Bendemolena's head. She made two holes for her ears and put it back on the kitten's head.

Mother Cat: Bendemolena, give me a hug.

Narrator: Did Bendemolena give her mother a bug or a rug? No, she gave her just what she wanted.

Bendemolena: A great big hug!

Sound and Stage Tips

About This play

This play is a story that you can read with your friends in a group or act out in front of an audience. Before you start reading, choose a part or parts you would like to read or act out. There are eight main parts in this play, so make sure you have readers for all the parts.

Reading the play

It is a good idea to practice reading the play to yourself before reading it as part of the group. Having your own book will allow you to keep the words in front of you as you move around the stage. Think about how the different characters might look. What expressions or gestures might they use? What might their voices sound like? How might they behave or move onstage?

Rehearsing the play

Rehearse the play a few times before you perform it for others. In *Bendemolena*, it is fun to act out the silly, mixed-up actions, e.g., ironing the meat and putting soap in the cake!

Remember that you are an actor as well as a reader. Your facial expressions and the way you move your body will really help the play come alive!

Using Your voice

Remember to speak out clearly and be careful not to read too quickly! The mixed-up words in *Bendemolena* are great fun to say and perform.

Remember to look at the audience and at the other actors, making sure that everyone can hear what you are saying.

Creating Sound Effects (FX)

You may like to add the sound of a ticking clock, using your mouth or two notes on a xylophone. You could also add some cat meows!

Sets and Props

Once you have read the play, make a list of the things you will need. Here are some ideas to help your performance. You may like to add some of your own.

- A pot for Bendemolena's head
- House scene: kitchen table, chairs, and door
- Street signs pointing to Mrs. Tabby's house and Bendemolena's house
- Tablecloth
- Pots and pans
- Picture of fish or soft toy fish
- Flowers for table
- Plastic box to use as a sink
- Plates, dishes

- Soap and grater
- Cake mix or bag of flour
- Mixing bowl
- Iron and ironing board
- Imaginary piece of meat!
- Clothes, scissors, needles, and thread
- Clock
- Toy riding-horse

Costumes

This play can be performed using simple costumes.
If you wish to dress up, you may find the following useful.
- Cat masks, ears, and whiskers for Mother Cat and Kittens
- Cape for Mr. Horse

Have fun!

Edel Wignell comes from a big family that is not quite as noisy as Bendemolena's!

The author's stories, scripts, verse, and articles have been published in many magazines, and she has written more than 60 books. She is interested in history, folklore, and fantasy. Edel Wignell likes writing humorous verse and is often inspired by the craziness of the English language: such phrases as "raining cats and dogs," "hoarse horse," and "mighty mites."

The author lives with her husband, Geoff, in Melbourne, Australia. For exercise, she power walks. She also likes bike riding, which gives you a clue to the pronunciation of her name: "Edel likes to pedal."